I LOVE ROCKS!

I LOVE ROCKS!

A Simple Guide to Using Crystals

Shelly Norris

Disclaimer: It is important that I say this - under no circumstances do I claim that these stones alone can heal you, fix you or guide you without taking your own action steps. The energy or frequency of these stones simply serve as a nudging reminder to use your own intuition and do what is best for you.

Dedication

With honor, I dedicate this book to the "Cool Guy," rock hound master, geology guru, tumbling genius. Without you, Shelly's Rock Shop wouldn't be. I thank you from the bottom of my heart.

Rock ON!

Acknowledgements

I would like to give a huge thank you to the Cool Guy for all the late nights you stayed up and packed my rock order. My customers and I are mighty grateful you did. Your stones are hands down the most gorgeous I've ever seen. I love how you take such pride in what you produce. I cannot thank you enough. I look forward to learning so much more from you. A heartfelt thank you is in order and a big hug next time I see you.

I want to give a giant shout out to a dear friend of mine, Suzan Thompson. She kindly offered to edit my book. She's brilliant and has a heart of gold. I'm super lucky to know you. Oh, and thank you for being there through the rough times. I hope your ear has healed from me talking it off. In deep and genuine gratitude for you. My cup runneth over.

Unknowingly, a beautiful and very helpful surprise came forward and offered to be my second edit. WOW! How truly blessed I am for your dedicated and continued efforts in helping me to edit and format my book correctly. Thank you Christy George for your patience and brilliant mind. I feel fortunate and grateful. Divine timing is truly divine.

Finally, I want to acknowledge all who encouraged me to make this book happen. Your support, excitement and high fives gave me what I needed to move forward. A true blessing of love, dedication and care from so many lovely people. My heart knows no bounds. Thank you!

Introduction

Hi! I'm Shelly Norris and I know a "Cool Guy." He's a master geologist, educator and my rock dealer. He's so cool that I believe he's the best rock tumbler in the U.S. and has the highest quality and largest tumbled stones this side of the Rocky Mountains. I am one lucky girl to know him. I keep him top secret and there are few who have caught a glimpse of him digging and collecting all over the Midwest.

It has come to my attention that brevity is key, and time is short in today's busy world. So here you go: straight from my rocks, my guides and me I give to you a rock book so easy to read, straight to the point, simple, fun, short and sweet. My rocks and I literally had a two-day rock party and what's in this book is the outcome.

The book is arranged in alphabetical order and each entry includes a brief description of the energy and message from each specific rock. There is also a list of chakras that tend to resonate with the energy of the stone. Be sure to check with your own intuition because the message of the rock and the chakra involved can shift, depending on what's going on for you.

Let's make this super easy and really fun. Over my many years working with rocks, I've learned to tune in to their unique frequencies and vibrations. The pages of this book reflect what I have learned. I'll share with you the simplest way I know how you can begin working with your rocks. Follow these few simple steps and record the information, insights, or feelings you gained on the pages in this book.

Step 1: At home or in a rock shop, look at the stones in front of you and pick up the first one that stands out. Remember: This is easy and fun, and it might just be the prettiest one!

Step 2: Read the description and see what part resonates with you. Begin there.

Step 3: Hold the rock tight, close your eyes, ask it any question. Start with everyday easy questions. For example: Should I have salad or fruit? Should I out go tonight or stay home?

Step 4: Slowly let the message drop in however that shows up for you. You may know, see, feel, or hear something right away or it may take a wee bit of time and practice. It can be as short as one word.

Don't give up! Let this be your simple beginning to using stones and your own intuition.

You, too, can learn to tune into these energies by practicing these basic steps I've created for you. Practicing will open you up to crystals in ways that will surprise you, astound you, and leave you saying, "You can't make this stuff up!"

For your convenience, pictures of all these stones (and many more) can be found on my Instagram, see page 245, or at:

https://www.instagram.com/shellynorris15/

Keep it simple, just have fun and rock on!

Amazonite

Communication with all, whether beyond, past or present is found in this stone. Hold tight and close your eyes. Ask - show me how to communicate with whoever has a message for me. Listen with closed eyes, an open heart and mind for visions or feelings of information to support you in the now. Practice this and you will be amazed. Also use to channel your favorite public speaker when you're on stage to help you blow your audience away!

Chakras: All

Fun Fact: Amazonite is found in many parts of the world. The highest quality, museum grade amazonite is found the Smoky Mountains of Virginia! I typically sell beautiful Russian amazonite and on occasion from Madagascar.

What insights, visions, words, understandings, perceptions, or awarenesses have I gained from my stone?

_____

_____

_____

_____

_____

_____

_____

_____

_____

_____

_____

_____

_____

_____

_____

Amethyst

Heal all levels of the energetic field: physical, emotional, mental and spiritual. You will thank yourself for adding this stone to your healing collection. Use when feeling off, out of balance, unclear, emotionally charged or in pain. Intention with this stone is key, using positive words with the results you seek. You are a divine being and worthy of all your heart's healthy desires.

Chakras: All

Fun Fact: Amethyst is purple quartz. Historically known as the stone of sobriety. Wine goblets were often made of amethyst to ward off drunkenness.

What insights, visions, words, understandings, perceptions, or awarenesses have I gained from my stone?

_____

_____

_____

_____

_____

_____

_____

_____

_____

_____

_____

_____

_____

_____

Ametrine

Use this stone to stimulate your intellect in situations that call for you to put your best foot forward. A stone that supports you in releasing old patterns around money so you can open up and receive all that Spirit has to offer you. Abundance is yours!

Chakras: All

Fun Fact: Ametrine is amethyst and citrine combined. Amethyst is purple quartz and citrine is yellow quartz. Its color comes from heat.

What insights, visions, words, understandings, perceptions, or awarenesses have I gained from my stone?

_____

_____

_____

_____

_____

_____

_____

_____

_____

_____

_____

_____

_____

_____

_____

Angelite

A high frequency stone that helps us connect and listen to our angels. It makes you feel more loved when feeling down, anxious or worried about something. Allows you to identify signs, symbols and metaphors given to you by your angels to let you know you're on the right path; a truly great feeling. Practice watching for the way your angels communicate with you while you go about your day.

Chakras: throat, third eye, crown

Fun Fact: Angelite belongs to the gypsum family and cannot go in water. It will dissolve over time.

What insights, visions, words, understandings, perceptions, or awarenesses have I gained from my stone?

_____

_____

_____

_____

_____

_____

_____

_____

_____

_____

_____

_____

_____

_____

Aquamarine

Raise your frequency and get what you want – that's how the Universe is intended to work! This high frequency stone is stable enough to help you see what is holding you back and what you need to move forward. A quiet mind can help you find the right forward movement to raise your frequency.

Chakras: solar plexus, throat, crown

Fun Fact: Aquamarine is in the beryl family. This means it is harder than quartz on the Mohs hardness scale of 1 – 10. Quartz is a 7 and beryl is an 8.

What insights, visions, words, understandings, perceptions, or awarenesses have I gained from my stone?

_____

_____

_____

_____

_____

_____

_____

_____

_____

_____

_____

_____

_____

_____

Aragonite

Do you have many desires you'd like to fulfill this lifetime? Look at this stone and notice that some will be filled quickly, and others will take longer. This is a stone of support while you navigate the waters of your desires. Be patient as you move along your path. If it doesn't feel right, adjust your course and just keep moving forward. Eventually you'll be on your path again. This stone shows you the way.

Chakras: All

Fun Fact: These are clusters of beautiful hexagonal column-shaped crystals. If you have blue aragonite it is likely dyed because white alone is not as appealing.

What insights, visions, words, understandings, perceptions, or awarenesses have I gained from my stone?

_____

_____

_____

_____

_____

_____

_____

_____

_____

_____

_____

_____

_____

_____

Birdseye Jasper

Aids in seeing things from a different perspective: see the forest through the trees or even the trees through the forest. Once your perspective shifts, even on the tiniest of things, you will start to see more harmony in the home and the workplace. Anger is diffused with this stone too. Hold it tight when feeling like a volcano about to explode.

Chakras: root, heart, throat, crown

Fun Fact: There are many types of orbicular japers. This is one of them.

What insights, visions, words, understandings, perceptions, or awarenesses have I gained from my stone?

_____

_____

_____

_____

_____

_____

_____

_____

_____

_____

_____

_____

_____

_____

Black & Brown
Zebra Lace Agate

Reminds us there is balance in all things even when we keep running into setbacks over and over. The peak is followed by the valley and the high is followed by the low, all the while allowing for ultimate flow in your life. This stone will support you and allow you to put a positive spin on just being, while traversing the peaks and valleys because they can often be tricky.

Chakras: root, solar plexus, heart

Fun Fact: Agates are generally translucent in nature. If they appear opaque, saw a thin slab and you will see light shining through. No access to a saw that slabs - trust me, if it's a true agate, it's translucent!

What insights, visions, words, understandings, perceptions, or awarenesses have I gained from my stone?

_____

_____

_____

_____

_____

_____

_____

_____

_____

_____

_____

_____

_____

_____

_____

Black Kyanite

The perfect stone for grounding and protection, allowing you to feel settled and safe when life gets hectic. Also aids in sweeping away the cobwebs of the mind for clearer thinking, leading to decision-making that feels right.

Chakras: root, solar plexus, third eye, crown

Fun Fact: This is a fragile stone and can often be called a broom or a fan. It looks very different from the blue and green kyanites.

What insights, visions, words, understandings, perceptions, or awarenesses have I gained from my stone?

_____

_____

_____

_____

_____

_____

_____

_____

_____

_____

_____

_____

_____

_____

Black Obsidian

This gentle, yet powerful stone helps us to remember the past, so we don't repeat the things that hurt ourselves or others. Use this stone to help you remember what's in your past that doesn't support you today, then clear out that which doesn't serve anymore. Seek professional help if necessary so you can be your best self this lifetime. Use this stone for discernment when listening to others about yourself. Everybody's got an opinion. You know YOU best!

Chakras: All

Fun Fact: Black obsidian is nature-made volcanic glass. Mostly black but has been known to come in other colors. The way to tell black obsidian from black onyx is to shine a bright flashlight through the stone and if you can see light it's obsidian. No light indicates onyx.

What insights, visions, words, understandings, perceptions, or awarenesses have I gained from my stone?

_____

_____

_____

_____

_____

_____

_____

_____

_____

_____

_____

_____

_____

_____

Black Tourmalinated Quartz

Even the sound of thunder can't shake this stone and its intentions to help you! The natural grounding of black tourmaline is amplified, magnified, and clarified by the high frequency of quartz. The energies of these stones combine to raise your vibration while keeping you deeply grounded. A great place from which to manifest. So manifest away with this amazing stone while keeping away all negativity!

Chakras: All

Fun Fact: This stone is clear or smoky quartz with black tourmaline needles that grew inside during the earth's creation process.

What insights, visions, words, understandings, perceptions, or awarenesses have I gained from my stone?

_____

_____

_____

_____

_____

_____

_____

_____

_____

_____

_____

_____

_____

_____

_____

Black Tourmaline

Protection times a million for all, especially the empathic ones. Removes negativity in all forms. Place this stone wherever you feel you need protection in all areas of your life. If someone breaks the barrier, whether physical or from the spirit world, place your hand on this stone, close your eyes and banish them from your energy field. Tell them out loud to keep their distance - especially from the spirit world. Be kinder to humans if you, can so hurt feelings don't get involved.

Chakras: All

Fun Fact: Most black tourmaline you see on the market is fairly fragile. The schorl crystal form of it is hard enough to make jewelry or carry in a pocket.

What insights, visions, words, understandings, perceptions, or awarenesses have I gained from my stone?

_____

_____

_____

_____

_____

_____

_____

_____

_____

_____

_____

_____

_____

_____

_____

Black & White
Zebra Lace Agate

Reminds us there is balance in all things. The up follows down and down follows up. A lifecycle of sorts. With the aid of this stone, step into the natural flow of your life with an open heart so you can become all you were meant to be this lifetime.

Chakras: root, solar plexus, heart

Fun Fact: Not only is there black and white zebra lace agate, we have zebra jasper and zebra quartz! Check out my Instagram for pictures.

What insights, visions, words, understandings, perceptions, or awarenesses have I gained from my stone?

_____

_____

_____

_____

_____

_____

_____

_____

_____

_____

_____

_____

_____

_____

_____

Bloodstone

A stone that supports overall good health. If you need encouragement in this area of your life this stone is a must for you. Sometimes you just know it is time to make a change, to better support your overall health. Let this stone help show you the way. Hold tight, close your eyes, and breath deep. Listen to what bloodstone has to tell you about your health and what things you can do to support your body. A great stone to gift others who suffer from illness and pain.

Chakras: All

Fun Fact: The Cool Guy also sells me orbicular bloodstone. The orbicular pattern are little circles on the stone. A rare and beautiful addition to your collection.

What insights, visions, words, understandings, perceptions, or awarenesses have I gained from my stone?

_____

_____

_____

_____

_____

_____

_____

_____

_____

_____

_____

_____

_____

_____

Blue Apatite

The stone of speaking your desires only to those who energetically support you. A powerful reminder that not all people in our lives support us on our journey. This stone will remind you to hold your goals and dreams close to the vest so the energy can build. When you're ready, you can send it out into the world with the support of those who encourage you.

Chakras: All; especially throat

Fun Fact: Blue apatite is mostly heat-treated green apatite, although not always. Is blue apatite real? Yes! Although most on the market are heat treated. You need to know and trust the source you buy from and ask the right questions. Then you'll know for sure.

What insights, visions, words, understandings, perceptions, or awarenesses have I gained from my stone?

_____

_____

_____

_____

_____

_____

_____

_____

_____

_____

_____

_____

_____

_____

_____

Blue Calcite

Speak your truth with love. This gentle frequency stone is your buddy. Use it with kindness and care towards others when speaking words they need to hear. Words are powerful and can help or hurt. It's your choice with this sweet stone and you will be encouraged to handle each situation with kindness.

Chakras: heart, throat

Fun Fact: A softer stone and easily scratched, especially if it's been shaped into a form such as a heart or palm stone.

What insights, visions, words, understandings, perceptions, or awarenesses have I gained from my stone?

_____

_____

_____

_____

_____

_____

_____

_____

_____

_____

_____

_____

_____

_____

_____

Blue Kyanite

Do you ever catch yourself speaking or thinking poorly about the most important person in the world...YOU? Allow this amazing stone to remind you to say and think about yourself with love, compassion and grace. Once you shift your conversation, it will spill over onto others to help them heal too. What a beautiful thing to witness!

Chakras: heart, throat

What insights, visions, words, understandings, perceptions, or awarenesses have I gained from my stone?

_____

_____

_____

_____

_____

_____

_____

_____

_____

_____

_____

_____

_____

_____

_____

Blue Lace Agate

One of our greatest needs is to feel heard. This stone encourages you to speak your truth always, even if your voice shakes and every bone in your body wants to run! Supports fearlessness when having important conversations. Aids in keeping your "cool" under pressure when it comes to communication in all forms.

Chakras: heart, throat

What insights, visions, words, understandings, perceptions, or awarenesses have I gained from my stone?

_____

_____

_____

_____

_____

_____

_____

_____

_____

_____

_____

_____

_____

_____

_____

Botswana Agate

A stone that enables one to see the light and dark in situations of the heart, mind and spirit and step into flow with the light. This stone enables clarity for decision-making; which is a helpful tool! Relieves depression with mindful effort, allowing one to see the big picture and take actionable steps towards improvement. Encourages exercise.

Chakras: root, heart, third eye, crown

What insights, visions, words, understandings, perceptions, or awarenesses have I gained from my stone?

_____

_____

_____

_____

_____

_____

_____

_____

_____

_____

_____

_____

_____

_____

Brecciated Jasper

This stone helps you put the pieces back together in any situation, allowing yourself to see the whole picture, rather than the fragments. A bird's eye view is a great way for a fresh start and perspective shift. A great stone to support your emotional and mental health.

Chakras: root, third eye, crown

Fun Fact: This stone was once solid red jasper. As the earth moves constantly it crushed the jasper replacing the cracks with silica which is quartz.

What insights, visions, words, understandings, perceptions, or awarenesses have I gained from my stone?

_____

_____

_____

_____

_____

_____

_____

_____

_____

_____

_____

_____

_____

_____

_____

Bullseye Chalcedony

Named after its colorful patterns, this stone helps one form an attitude of, "Get it done!" Aids in releasing the energy of procrastination to the energy of "let's begin and complete what needs to be done." Feel a sense of accomplishment when you carry this stone.

Chakras: sacral, solar plexus, throat, third eye

Fun Fact: Fun Fact: This stone is mined by the Cool Guy himself!

Chalcedony pronounced:
Cal-said-knee

What insights, visions, words, understandings, perceptions, or awarenesses have I gained from my stone?

_____

_____

_____

_____

_____

_____

_____

_____

_____

_____

_____

_____

_____

Bumblebee Jasper

How important is it for you to show up daily as your best self? YOU are #1; always have been and always will be. Let this stone remind you how important it is to show up and be your best self because it will rub off on others, allowing them to also show up and be their best self. The world needs more of YOU when you are your best self, for you are a masterpiece! In deep gratitude for you. Thank you!

Chakras: solar plexus, heart

Fun Fact: Mined in Indonesia.

What insights, visions, words, understandings, perceptions, or awarenesses have I gained from my stone?

_____

_____

_____

_____

_____

_____

_____

_____

_____

_____

_____

_____

_____

_____

Butterstone

This is about your skin, the largest organ in your body. Everything you do for your body inside and out shows up in your skin. Use with care as you create new ways to soften and clear up all that doesn't serve. Health is of your utmost importance now. This stone will support you in making good choices that support your body.

Chakras: solar plexus, heart, crown

Fun Fact: This stone is 2,500 million years older than the dinosaur.

What insights, visions, words, understandings, perceptions, or awarenesses have I gained from my stone?

_____

_____

_____

_____

_____

_____

_____

_____

_____

_____

_____

_____

_____

_____

Carnelian

Aids in giving birth to new ideas, all the while bringing in the right people to help you move your ideas forward. Keeps away the naysayers. Creativity abounds when working with this stone and Spirit for guidance.

Chakras: sacral, heart

Fun Fact: This stone is an agate. The color of this stone is often deepened by adding heat to the finishing process, but not the Cool Guy's carnelian. It's all natural.

What insights, visions, words, understandings, perceptions, or awarenesses have I gained from my stone?

_____

_____

_____

_____

_____

_____

_____

_____

_____

_____

_____

_____

_____

_____

Celestite

A super-high frequency stone that helps you connect with your angels. Your angels are pure love and can only be just that. When you're feeling down, alone or depressed call on your angels to lift you up using the frequency of this stone. Know you are lovingly supported.

Chakras: heart, crown

What insights, visions, words, understandings, perceptions, or awarenesses have I gained from my stone?

_____

_____

_____

_____

_____

_____

_____

_____

_____

_____

_____

_____

_____

_____

Charoite

A high frequency and powerful stone with a hint of sass. This stone will bring out the sassy side of you in a way that makes you feel beautiful and courageous. Depression be gone when using this stone, for sassy and depression don't mix. Feel your oats again!

Chakras: root, solar plexus, throat, third eye

Fun Fact: A beautiful Russian purple stone often used in jewelry.

What insights, visions, words, understandings, perceptions, or awarenesses have I gained from my stone?

_____

_____

_____

_____

_____

_____

_____

_____

_____

_____

_____

_____

_____

_____

Cheetah Jasper

When you're ready to run forward fast in your life, this stone shows up. Hold the stone and connect all the dots of your life, knowing what's truth and what will be left behind. An abundant stone of truth for only you.

Chakras: solar plexus

What insights, visions, words, understandings, perceptions, or awarenesses have I gained from my stone?

_____

_____

_____

_____

_____

_____

_____

_____

_____

_____

_____

_____

_____

_____

_____

Chevron Amethyst

One notch above regular amethyst; because you can point the chevrons in the direction of the needed healing. Heal all levels of the energetic field: physical, emotional, mental and spiritual. You will thank yourself for adding this stone to your healing collection! Use when feeling off, out of balance, unclear, emotionally charged or in pain. Intention is key! Use positive words with the results you seek. You are a divine being and worthy of all your heart desires.

Chakras: All

What insights, visions, words, understandings, perceptions, or awarenesses have I gained from my stone?

_____

_____

_____

_____

_____

_____

_____

_____

_____

_____

_____

_____

_____

_____

Chiastolite

Aids in helping you open your third eye so you can "see" the answers you've been seeking. Our third eye is super powerful when used to guide us on our path. While in meditation use your third eye to see your next right steps. It's guaranteed to work with practice. Also use the power of the four cardinal directions. This stone recommends you start your journey in the east as a novice and move clockwise as you grow with the information from your third eye. A great Shaman's stone.

Chakras: solar plexus, third eye, crown

Fun Fact: Also called andalusite.

What insights, visions, words, understandings, perceptions, or awarenesses have I gained from my stone?

_____

_____

_____

_____

_____

_____

_____

_____

_____

_____

_____

_____

_____

_____

Chinese Writing Stone

Aids in understanding others' perspectives while standing in your power and opening your mind and heart for better understanding. An energetic shift, all the while feeling supported, as you release anger during related situations connected to another's perspective.

Chakras: root, throat, third eye

Fun Fact: Mined in California, not China.

What insights, visions, words, understandings, perceptions, or awarenesses have I gained from my stone?

_____

_____

_____

_____

_____

_____

_____

_____

_____

_____

_____

_____

_____

_____

Chrysocolla

Step into beautiful movement and alignment with your heart's desires with this beauty! Listen, act, and reap the rewards while using this stone. Support yourself meaningfully and magically. Use this stone daily, either by holding it or meditating on it for answers to your next right step. Then step forward!

Chakras: All

What insights, visions, words, understandings, perceptions, or awarenesses have I gained from my stone?

_____

_____

_____

_____

_____

_____

_____

_____

_____

_____

_____

_____

_____

_____

Chrysoprase

A powerful heart healer when it comes to relationships of all kinds. Allows us to love more freely even when we feel closed. Hold this stone and feel your heart open, letting it guide you to make the right choice regarding relationships - even if it's the hard choice! Energetically, some relationships will stay, and some will go. Let them be exactly what they are and don't force it. Let go and be free.

Chakras: root, heart

What insights, visions, words, understandings, perceptions, or awarenesses have I gained from my stone?

_____

_____

_____

_____

_____

_____

_____

_____

_____

_____

_____

_____

_____

Chytha

Aids in a more disciplined way of "doing" life. A strong stone with a trace of luck, sure to bring about positive changes. Relieves anxiety with a positive and focused mind.

Chakras: root, sacral, solar plexus, heart, third eye

Fun Fact: The light green is serpentine, and the dark green is jade. From China.

What insights, visions, words, understandings, perceptions, or awarenesses have I gained from my stone?

_____

_____

_____

_____

_____

_____

_____

_____

_____

_____

_____

_____

_____

_____

Cinnabar

Money, money, money! We all need money to live our best lives in pursuit of helping others as well as ourselves. Put this stone in your cash drawer or wallet. Watch the magic happen. You are worthy of any vacation or shopping spree you desire too! Taking action is necessary.

Chakras: All

Fun Fact: Also called cinnabrite. I've had one of these in my cash drawer since the inception of my business, and it continues to thrive and grow!

What insights, visions, words, understandings, perceptions, or awarenesses have I gained from my stone?

_____

_____

_____

_____

_____

_____

_____

_____

_____

_____

_____

_____

_____

_____

_____

Citrine

Citrine was historically known as the merchant's stone and can be used for powerful money intentions. Imagine, with your mind's eye, your bank account, wallet, and pockets fill right up with money. Aids in clearing out any and all emotional and mental blocks allowing you to take massive action towards your financial prosperity. Action is key.

Chakras: root, sacral, solar plexus, crown

Fun Fact: Most people don't think of citrine as quartz, but it is. Citrine is yellow quartz. Sometimes amethyst can be heated in the finishing process to turn yellow and sold as citrine rather than amethyst.

What insights, visions, words, understandings, perceptions, or awarenesses have I gained from my stone?

_____

_____

_____

_____

_____

_____

_____

_____

_____

_____

_____

_____

_____

_____

_____

Clear Quartz

Intentions are everything, whether positive or negative. Use this stone with powerful and clear intentions. This stone will amplify, magnify and clarify whatever is going on in your life whether helpful or destructive. This stone does not discern for you; that is your job. It can only give you what you put out there. Be mindful and keep it positive.

Chakras: crown

Fun Fact: The highest quality quartz comes from Arkansas and Brazil. Quartz carries such a stable frequency that it is used to complete a full circuit in our electronic devices.

What insights, visions, words, understandings, perceptions, or awarenesses have I gained from my stone?

_____

_____

_____

_____

_____

_____

_____

_____

_____

_____

_____

_____

_____

_____

Coprolite

This stone is a great reminder to eat healthier: more plants, fruits and nuts. When you hit that wall and slide into fast or faster food, grab this stone as your cue to not get upset with yourself and let it just be a gentle reminder to do better next time. Love yourself and all will be right with your world.

Chakras: All

Fun Fact: Fossil dinosaur poop. (It's now a rock so don't worry!)

What insights, visions, words, understandings, perceptions, or awarenesses have I gained from my stone?

_____

_____

_____

_____

_____

_____

_____

_____

_____

_____

_____

_____

_____

_____

_____

Crater Jasper

Wishes do come true with this sweet stone! Great for all ages from 5 to 95 years old. It will stand the test of time as it continues to grant your wishes. Its sweet energy will continue to grow with you as you step into new and exciting areas of your life. A great pocket stone used as a reminder to "ask for what you want" even if it's just a close parking space!

Chakras: All

What insights, visions, words, understandings, perceptions, or awarenesses have I gained from my stone?

_____

_____

_____

_____

_____

_____

_____

_____

_____

_____

_____

_____

_____

_____

Crazy Lace Agate

When life gets overwhelming, follow the design patterns of this pretty stone with your eyes or trace it with your finger. It reminds you to slow down and follow your best path, supporting you on the mental, emotional, physical and spiritual levels. This stone takes you deep onto your path through all the twists, turns, and traffic detours. Go with the flow of the stone's patterns and adjust accordingly.

Chakras: All

What insights, visions, words, understandings, perceptions, or awarenesses have I gained from my stone?

_____

_____

_____

_____

_____

_____

_____

_____

_____

_____

_____

_____

_____

_____

Dalmatian Jasper

A stone of gentle love. It's the type that sneaks up on you unexpectedly - whether from a past, current or future relationship. Wishes do come true with this stone. Wish for matters dealing with the heart. See and feel them happening. Love is just a sweet kiss away. Connect the dots on this stone to the healthy and good times you've had with another to form a whole new understanding of what it is you truly want this lifetime.

Chakras: All

What insights, visions, words, understandings, perceptions, or awarenesses have I gained from my stone?

_____

_____

_____

_____

_____

_____

_____

_____

_____

_____

_____

_____

_____

_____

Dragon Stone

Dragon Stone makes it easier to free your inner warrior while remaining grounded. Use this stone with powerful intention and purpose when channeling your inner warrior. Kindness and grace are still important, so focus on the green epidote in this stone and you will be supported with the red jasper for the warrior self.

Chakras: root, heart

What insights, visions, words, understandings, perceptions, or awarenesses have I gained from my stone?

_____

_____

_____

_____

_____

_____

_____

_____

_____

_____

_____

_____

_____

_____

Emerald

Emerald is a symbol of wealth and prosperity, especially money. Wealth and prosperity can spill over into other areas of your life with powerful intentions. Where do you want to see more wealth, more prosperity in your life? Hold this stone loosely, for too tight and you may step into desperation, an energy that repels what it is we seek.

Chakras: All

What insights, visions, words, understandings, perceptions, or awarenesses have I gained from my stone?

_____

_____

_____

_____

_____

_____

_____

_____

_____

_____

_____

_____

_____

_____

Fluorite

A brilliant meditation and focus aid. The beauty of this stone is so mesmerizing that it's hard not to hold it in natural light and just stare! Allow this stone to help you improve upon your meditation skills. Seek the answers you've been searching for. Spirit loves to communicate through its translucency while dropping in information that you seek.

Chakras: heart, throat, third eye, crown

What insights, visions, words, understandings, perceptions, or awarenesses have I gained from my stone?

_____

_____

_____

_____

_____

_____

_____

_____

_____

_____

_____

_____

_____

_____

_____

Garden Quartz

How do you view the world you live in? With love or anger? Allow this unique stone help you send more love into the world so we can all heal. Go inside this stone via your third eye and meditation. You'll be able to view a world so beautiful and perfect it opens your heart to all things, ideas and concepts that need healing and understanding. While you're in the stone feel free to grab some nuggets of information for yourself too! All it takes is practice!

Chakras: heart, third eye

What insights, visions, words, understandings, perceptions, or awarenesses have I gained from my stone?

_____

_____

_____

_____

_____

_____

_____

_____

_____

_____

_____

_____

_____

_____

_____

Garnet

An uplifting stone, garnet assists in self-love while achieving profound deep relaxation. It reminds you to treat yourself to something special that will relax your mind, body and spirit.

Chakras: heart

What insights, visions, words, understandings, perceptions, or awarenesses have I gained from my stone?

_____

_____

_____

_____

_____

_____

_____

_____

_____

_____

_____

_____

_____

_____

Golden Healer Quartz

Heal the healers, mothers, fathers and all who take care of others. Healing golden and white light surround you while you go through your day with this stone. This light comes from the heavens and is angelic in nature so it's a soft gentle energy that heals. Call on your angels every time you see, feel, or carry this stone.

Chakras: heart, throat, third eye, crown

What insights, visions, words, understandings, perceptions, or awarenesses have I gained from my stone?

_____

_____

_____

_____

_____

_____

_____

_____

_____

_____

_____

_____

_____

_____

_____

_____

Golden Tiger's Eye

This stone supports the masculine in all of us, male or female. It encourages you to "get yourself out there, stand tall, stand proud, be all of who you are, be loud, be daring, be courageous and most of all be heard." Speak so others can hear you. You are supported in using the right words for each conversation. Keeping this stone close brings admiration your way.

Chakras: solar plexus, crown

Fun Fact: While this stone is golden, there is a red tiger's eye and a blue tiger's eye. The blue is called hawk eye.

What insights, visions, words, understandings, perceptions, or awarenesses have I gained from my stone?

_____

_____

_____

_____

_____

_____

_____

_____

_____

_____

_____

_____

_____

_____

Goldstone

Use this beautiful stone to connect with the energy of the heavens and mother earth - bringing that energy into your creative center and sending it out into the world. The sparkly copper flecks open you to imagination on a higher level. Seek creative ideas to build the life want now using this stone. Share your creative ideas with positive and supportive people.

Chakras: All

Fun Fact: This stone is manmade glass and comes in gold, blue and green. The sparkles are copper flecks.

What insights, visions, words, understandings, perceptions, or awarenesses have I gained from my stone?

_____

_____

_____

_____

_____

_____

_____

_____

_____

_____

_____

_____

_____

_____

Green Calcite

A sweet, high frequency, loving stone. Green calcite is the color of your heart chakra. Allow this beauty to open you to your highest good in all areas of your life; especially when it comes to any health problems. You will see what you need to do with the support of this stone. Love is the answer.

Chakras: heart

What insights, visions, words, understandings, perceptions, or awarenesses have I gained from my stone?

Green Moss Agate

This gorgeous stone is a must-add to your collection! It connects you with the plant and animal kingdoms, as well as the fairies. And who doesn't love the fairies? Sit quietly in nature with this stone and just watch and listen. Journal what you see, hear and feel. You will be surprised. Share with a friend who understands.

Chakras: All

What insights, visions, words, understandings, perceptions, or awarenesses have I gained from my stone?

_____

_____

_____

_____

_____

_____

_____

_____

_____

_____

_____

_____

_____

_____

Green Spiderweb Jasper

It is within the webs we weave that we find our truth. Keep weaving, by living your truthful life, with this stone to help guide you towards your next right step fearless and brave. Your complete truth awaits you.

Chakras: sacral, solar plexus

Fun Fact: This stone is mined by the Cool Guy himself!

What insights, visions, words, understandings, perceptions, or awarenesses have I gained from my stone?

_____

_____

_____

_____

_____

_____

_____

_____

_____

_____

_____

_____

_____

_____

Green Tree Agate

Joy! Are you seeking more joy in your life? The kind that lasts for more than a day or two? This stone wards away depression – thankfully, because we sure don't have time for that! It also wards off any shenanigans in the workplace and with family because, if you feel joy, the people around you will too. What a beautiful thing to share with others!

Chakras: root, solar plexus, heart

What insights, visions, words, understandings, perceptions, or awarenesses have I gained from my stone?

_____

_____

_____

_____

_____

_____

_____

_____

_____

_____

_____

_____

_____

_____

_____

Green Zebra Lace Agate

A great stability stone while on the job or at home. Hold tight to feel your heart open when feeling frustrated or anxious as you calm and comfort yourself with the energy you desire. It is high time to start feeling yourself again with this beauty!

Chakras: root, heart

What insights, visions, words, understandings, perceptions, or awarenesses have I gained from my stone?

_____

_____

_____

_____

_____

_____

_____

_____

_____

_____

_____

_____

_____

_____

_____

Hawk Eye

The throat chakra is blue, and the solar plexus is yellow. This stone is a deep, dark blue with hints of yellow, thus making it very formidable. Allow this stone to motivate you to want to communicate by being straight forward (not wishy washy) - all the while using compassion and kindness. Strong words are important and can help or hurt. Use mindfully.

Chakras: solar plexus, throat

Fun Fact: Also called as blue tiger's eye.

What insights, visions, words, understandings, perceptions, or awarenesses have I gained from my stone?

_____

_____

_____

_____

_____

_____

_____

_____

_____

_____

_____

_____

_____

_____

Hematite

A super powerful grounding stone. Keep nearby in a pocket, car or even during mediation. Feel yourself sink into Mother Earth as she holds you tight. A calming stone too!

Chakras: root, heart, third eye

What insights, visions, words, understandings, perceptions, or awarenesses have I gained from my stone?

_____

_____

_____

_____

_____

_____

_____

_____

_____

_____

_____

_____

_____

_____

_____

_____

Hematoid Quartz

Your passions will burn with desire while holding this powerful stone. Hold tight and allow your feelings to flow from your heart and mind into a journal. Then, take this energy and send it out into the Universe so your spiritual team can help what you desire show up in unexpected ways. I can see the smoke now from the fire you lit to send your passions up into the heavens! Have fun manifesting!

Chakras: All

Fun Fact: Also called fire quartz. The reddish color in this quartz is caused by iron oxide.

What insights, visions, words, understandings, perceptions, or awarenesses have I gained from my stone?

_____

_____

_____

_____

_____

_____

_____

_____

_____

_____

_____

_____

_____

_____

Howlite

Howlite is a stone to help you face the truth about your life. Where are you in agreement with your life? Notice the lines on the howlite and see how they relate to your own personal life. Follow them, journal what you discover and move your life forward in dynamic ways. Be true to yourself.

Chakras: All

Fun Fact: The true form of howlite is white with light grey lines. Other colors of howlite have been dyed.

What insights, visions, words, understandings, perceptions, or awarenesses have I gained from my stone?

_____

_____

_____

_____

_____

_____

_____

_____

_____

_____

_____

_____

_____

_____

Hypersthene

A powerful MAGIC stone! Hold this stone while focusing on your intentions and with a flick of your wrist send them up towards the heavens. You will be heard immediately! Check in with the energy of your intention and spiritual alignment. The more aligned you are, the faster they will show up. Let your magical heart lead the way. Take action now step by step by step. You've got this!

Chakras: All

What insights, visions, words, understandings, perceptions, or awarenesses have I gained from my stone?

_____

_____

_____

_____

_____

_____

_____

_____

_____

_____

_____

_____

_____

_____

_____

Iron Pyrite

Money! We all deserve exactly what we want in life - including money. There is no shame in this. It takes money for us to be able to do the things we need to do. Put your pyrite on a $20, $100 bill or a check with the amount you desire. Send your intentions out into the Universe and take action. The key here is **action**. Do something that supports your intentions. We all deserve a dream vacation and then some!

Chakras: All

Fun Fact: Also called fool's gold.

What insights, visions, words, understandings, perceptions, or awarenesses have I gained from my stone?

_____

_____

_____

_____

_____

_____

_____

_____

_____

_____

_____

_____

_____

_____

Jade

Luck is always on your side when it comes to issues of the heart and wallet. Jade reminds you to stay alert when your angels are trying to get your attention. Your angels are pure love and always want what's best for you. See your luck turn around quickly.

Chakras: Heart, Crown

What insights, visions, words, understandings, perceptions, or awarenesses have I gained from my stone?

_____

_____

_____

_____

_____

_____

_____

_____

_____

_____

_____

_____

_____

_____

Jet

Allows you to feel grounded while remaining light in body, mind and spirit. Helps you see into the past for growth today. Supports healing and understanding past lives and childhood issues accordingly. Encourage more joy.

Chakras: root, solar plexus, third eye

What insights, visions, words, understandings, perceptions, or awarenesses have I gained from my stone?

_____

_____

_____

_____

_____

_____

_____

_____

_____

_____

_____

_____

_____

_____

K2 Blue

Close your eyes and hold this stone. Can you see the top of the mountain? That's your mountain. The one you choose to climb this lifetime. Is it worth it? Heck YES, it is! Go get'em tiger!

Chakras: sacral, solar plexus, heart, third eye

Fun Fact: This stone comes from the second tallest mountain in the world. It's called K2 and located in Pakistan. It is blue azurite that grew on granite.

What insights, visions, words, understandings,
perceptions, or awarenesses have I gained from
my stone?

_____

_____

_____

_____

_____

_____

_____

_____

_____

_____

_____

_____

_____

_____

Kambaba Jasper

Aids in bravery and courage to be your dynamic self. Supports the body's frequency for faster healing, all the while releasing anger towards others. Anger causes pain and disease. Hold this stone close so you can then let go, forgive and heal.

Chakras: root, heart, crown

What insights, visions, words, understandings, perceptions, or awarenesses have I gained from my stone?

_____

_____

_____

_____

_____

_____

_____

_____

_____

_____

_____

_____

_____

_____

Kunzite

A sweet stone with a super high frequency. The level of your personal vibration is important. Raise your frequency to get what you want. A stone to remind you to do the things you love and let go of the things that drag you down. It gives you that feeling of "My cup runneth over."

Chakras: heart

What insights, visions, words, understandings, perceptions, or awarenesses have I gained from my stone?

_____

_____

_____

_____

_____

_____

_____

_____

_____

_____

_____

_____

_____

_____

Labradorite

Open and connect your heart with your mind using this magical stone. Alignment is key. Once in alignment, magical flow naturally occurs. Watch for what you've been asking for to start showing up easily and in surprisingly perfect ways you never would have expected. Share with others your experiences with this stone and it will help them too!

Chakras: All

What insights, visions, words, understandings, perceptions, or awarenesses have I gained from my stone?

_____

_____

_____

_____

_____

_____

_____

_____

_____

_____

_____

_____

_____

_____

Lapis Lazuli

Aahhhhh! The stone of ultimate intuition.
We all have powerful intuition and often
overlook what our gut knows before our brain
takes over. It happens so fast. Allow this
stone to teach you, through practice, to pay
attention to your gut intuition. You will be
super happy you did! Lapis is also the stone
of royalty that makes you feel like a
king/queen, prince/princess or god/goddess.

Chakras: solar plexus, heart, third eye, crown

What insights, visions, words, understandings, perceptions, or awarenesses have I gained from my stone?

_____

_____

_____

_____

_____

_____

_____

_____

_____

_____

_____

_____

_____

_____

_____

Leopard Skin Jasper

Use this gentle yet brave stone to help you pull yourself up by your bootstraps for a better today. This stone gives you the courage to do so, all the while being kind to yourself. Gentle and brave are a powerful force together. For today, choose the energies this stone supports.

Chakras: root, solar plexus, heart

What insights, visions, words, understandings, perceptions, or awarenesses have I gained from my stone?

_____

_____

_____

_____

_____

_____

_____

_____

_____

_____

_____

_____

_____

_____

_____

Lepidolite

Calm, calm, calm. An amazing anti-anxiety stone that will reduce the feeling of crazy in your whole body! This stone has natural lithium which is good for everyone at one time or another. Whether you need it every second of the day or only once in a while. It's the stone of calm. Hold it tight and rub it, then notice how your mood shifts.

Chakras: All

Fun Fact: This stone has natural lithium from the earth.

What insights, visions, words, understandings, perceptions, or awarenesses have I gained from my stone?

_____

_____

_____

_____

_____

_____

_____

_____

_____

_____

_____

_____

_____

_____

Malachite

Do you ever feel like you don't know which direction to go next - especially when it comes to your physical health or mental health? This badass stone will help you figure it out AND give you the strength to do what needs to be done! You'll be directed to see the right doctors, holistic practitioners, counselors, life coaches, or dieticians. Whatever it is... you will have the strength to do it. You will feel brave and completely ready while holding this stone tightly. You've got this!

Chakras: All

What insights, visions, words, understandings, perceptions, or awarenesses have I gained from my stone?

_____

_____

_____

_____

_____

_____

_____

_____

_____

_____

_____

_____

_____

_____

_____

Midnight Jasper

Wishes are important. Send your wishes into the heavens with this stone and watch them stick to all the stars while an angel swoops down and picks one up. Our angels love to help us achieve all of our wishes. So hold this stone tight as your wishes come true, then give thanks to all who helped.

Chakras: sacral, heart, throat, third eye, crown

Fun Fact: Also called Onyx.

What insights, visions, words, understandings, perceptions, or awarenesses have I gained from my stone?

_____

_____

_____

_____

_____

_____

_____

_____

_____

_____

_____

_____

_____

_____

_____

Mookaite Jasper

Aids in seeing the beauty in everything even during the dark times. Gaze at this stone and glimpse into your future with eyes wide open all the while feeling fearless. Move forward now because you are ready. Take intentional action.

Chakras: All

Fun Fact: From the Mooka River in Australia.

What insights, visions, words, understandings, perceptions, or awarenesses have I gained from my stone?

_____

_____

_____

_____

_____

_____

_____

_____

_____

_____

_____

_____

_____

_____

_____

_____

Moonstone

Balance - a deeper connection to the Divine Feminine and the Divine Masculine is obtained with this stone. We all have feminine and masculine energies within us and it's important to connect to both. Let this stone aid you in getting in touch with these energies so you can feel balanced from within. A powerful feeling for a happy life!

Chakras: All

What insights, visions, words, understandings, perceptions, or awarenesses have I gained from my stone?

_____

_____

_____

_____

_____

_____

_____

_____

_____

_____

_____

_____

_____

_____

Mugglestone

Are you this? Or that? Choose a side and play ball. Don't let the naysayers get you down! Ground yourself with this stone so you can be your truest self and the badass you were born to be. Allow this stone to be that reminder to you when you are feeling stuck in the middle. Eat some ice cream (or do something you enjoy) just be done with the "stuck". Imagine putting the "stuck" into this stone and watch it absorb it away.

Chakras: All

What insights, visions, words, understandings, perceptions, or awarenesses have I gained from my stone?

_____

_____

_____

_____

_____

_____

_____

_____

_____

_____

_____

_____

_____

_____

_____

Noble Serpentine

Heal yourself. Heal others. This stone is perfect for both. Whatever type of healing you desire, even jealousy or envy, can be found with this stone. Feel great, look great, and smile your best smile. Smiling heals and this stone also reminds you to smile. Say cheese!

Chakras: root, heart, crown

Fun Fact: Also called Healerite.

What insights, visions, words, understandings, perceptions, or awarenesses have I gained from my stone?

_____

_____

_____

_____

_____

_____

_____

_____

_____

_____

_____

_____

_____

Ocean Jasper

Move with the current of beauty and grace. This super-sweet stone is so beautiful that one can't help but fall captive to its energies. Having this stone nearby ensures kindness on all levels and in all areas of your life. Anger, worry, frustration... be gone!

Chakras: All

What insights, visions, words, understandings, perceptions, or awarenesses have I gained from my stone?

_____

_____

_____

_____

_____

_____

_____

_____

_____

_____

_____

_____

_____

_____

_____

_____

Opalite

No matter where you are, know you are always connected to Divine Guidance. Achieve greatness by following in the footsteps of the people you admire: both past and present. Learn from their mistakes and grow from their successes. A great stone for those seeking guidance in their lives now.

Chakras: Crown, solar plexus

Fun Fact: This stone is manmade glass permanently bonded with metals giving it that iridescent fiery glow.

What insights, visions, words, understandings, perceptions, or awarenesses have I gained from my stone?

_____

_____

_____

_____

_____

_____

_____

_____

_____

_____

_____

_____

_____

_____

Orange Calcite

May you dream while awake and asleep with this highly creative stone. Your dreams of creating new ideas, followed by action is what is needed now. Use this stone in manifesting grids about making your ideas become reality. Keep the energy of this beauty close to you so your body will start to vibe with the stone's frequency.

Chakras: sacral, solar plexus, third eye

What insights, visions, words, understandings, perceptions, or awarenesses have I gained from my stone?

_____

_____

_____

_____

_____

_____

_____

_____

_____

_____

_____

_____

_____

_____

Peridot

This beautiful stone aids us in seeing the sweeter side of life when times get tough. It helps us to appreciate being alive right here and now and to know the best is yet to come. Also reminds us to count our blessings. If it's your birthstone - even better!

Chakras: heart, crown

What insights, visions, words, understandings, perceptions, or awarenesses have I gained from my stone?

_____

_____

_____

_____

_____

_____

_____

_____

_____

_____

_____

_____

_____

_____

Petrified Wood

Do you ever feel alive inside? Dead inside? Both are is a natural part of life. We all experience it. Step into flow and connect to Spirit with this stone when you need to feel alive again: the type of alive that you feel with wild abandon to dance it out. Hold this stone tight to feel beautiful too!

Chakras: sacral, solar plexus, heart, crown

Fun Fact: These stones are mined by the Cool Guy himself! I carry two types of petrified wood: conifer from Oregon and the other from Arizona.

What insights, visions, words, understandings, perceptions, or awarenesses have I gained from my stone?

_____

_____

_____

_____

_____

_____

_____

_____

_____

_____

_____

_____

_____

_____

Pink Opal

A frequency so soft and sweet it's angelic. Let this stone help you connect to your angels. Remember you are never alone - your angels are always around! Aids in helping those who feel alone or left out by reminding them to summon their angels in a moment's notice to feel their high vibrational love immediately and on command. That's how our angels like it!

Chakras: heart

What insights, visions, words, understandings, perceptions, or awarenesses have I gained from my stone?

_____

_____

_____

_____

_____

_____

_____

_____

_____

_____

_____

_____

_____

_____

Pink Tourmaline in Quartz

Believe in the sweetness of others' hearts - even when it comes to family members and co-workers. A powerful, yet soft stone aiding you to be powerful and soft at the same time with others who are part of your life.

Chakras: heart, crown

What insights, visions, words, understandings, perceptions, or awarenesses have I gained from my stone?

_____

_____

_____

_____

_____

_____

_____

_____

_____

_____

_____

_____

_____

_____

Pinolite

What do you see in this stone? Allow this stone to guide you every time you look at it from a different angle. Aids in reminding us to look at life from more than one view. Perspective is the key.

Chakras: sacral, third eye, crown

Fun Fact: This stone comes from only one place in the world in Austria: the Central Eastern Alps. It was mined during World War II for its high manganese content used in the production of iron and steel.

What insights, visions, words, understandings, perceptions, or awarenesses have I gained from my stone?

_____

_____

_____

_____

_____

_____

_____

_____

_____

_____

_____

_____

_____

_____

Piranha Agate

This high-quality agate comes to us from Brazil. Hold it up to the light to see all the natural layers of the agate. Allow this stone to help you stand tall and proud when confronting authority figures. It reminds you to fight for what is right in any given situation concerning work, family and legal matters. You are heard.

Chakras: root, solar plexus, throat

What insights, visions, words, understandings, perceptions, or awarenesses have I gained from my stone?

_____

_____

_____

_____

_____

_____

_____

_____

_____

_____

_____

_____

_____

_____

Polka Dot Agate

Aids in recalling the best memories of our childhood and encourages us to remember the good feelings associated with those memories. Helps us to release any painful memories we choose for emotional growth and freedom. Feel **FREE** again with this sweet stone! Lock in the goodness that comes with wild abandon, just like a child. Also reminds us to treat ourselves like we would treat a child: with kindness, compassion and love.

Chakras: All

What insights, visions, words, understandings, perceptions, or awarenesses have I gained from my stone?

_____

_____

_____

_____

_____

_____

_____

_____

_____

_____

_____

_____

_____

_____

Polychrome Jasper

Allows us to see the unique beauty in others without judgement. Heals the heart of past hurts during times we were judged. Permits hurt feelings to mend by removing the old energy out of our body and allowing positive energy to fill in.

Chakras: root, sacral, solar plexus, heart

What insights, visions, words, understandings, perceptions, or awarenesses have I gained from my stone?

_____

_____

_____

_____

_____

_____

_____

_____

_____

_____

_____

_____

_____

_____

Porcelain Jasper

A reminder to treat ourselves as we would treat a child. Kindness and compassion for self with a touch of gentleness is a sure-fire way to remember that you are a gift to this world. With this stone, let your bright light shine so everyone can see you and appreciate all of your talents and gifts, because YOU have remembered how precious you are!

Chakras: All

What insights, visions, words, understandings, perceptions, or awarenesses have I gained from my stone?

_____

_____

_____

_____

_____

_____

_____

_____

_____

_____

_____

_____

_____

_____

_____

Prasiolite

This stone is so powerful it can do just about anything you intend as long as it's positive and with heart. It aids in remembering your dreams whether your eyes are open or closed. This stone can cut the energic cords that tie two people together and release the weight of that negative energy. Do this with vivid intention. Step into your unique self with this stone.

Chakras: All

Fun Fact: Also known as green amethyst.

What insights, visions, words, understandings, perceptions, or awarenesses have I gained from my stone?

_____

_____

_____

_____

_____

_____

_____

_____

_____

_____

_____

_____

_____

_____

_____

Prehnite

Seek and you shall find your body's health and your mental health. Reminds you to do good things for the body, mind and spirit. Unhealthy emotions are captured in this stone too, so give them over for massive healing. Do the work for a healthy outcome. With this stone close, by consider journaling that which doesn't serve you and then burn the pages with the intention of seeing them float into non-existence.

Chakras: All

What insights, visions, words, understandings, perceptions, or awarenesses have I gained from my stone?

_____

_____

_____

_____

_____

_____

_____

_____

_____

_____

_____

_____

_____

_____

_____

Prehnite with Epidote

Healers of any type need healing too! Therefore, this stone aids in jogging the memory to help you take care of yourself. We get one life in this body. Use this stone to help you make it the best it can be. Stand for your beliefs in a way that supports you and those around you. Keeps you on track and focused. A fantastic stone to include in your life!

Chakras: All

What insights, visions, words, understandings, perceptions, or awarenesses have I gained from my stone?

_____

_____

_____

_____

_____

_____

_____

_____

_____

_____

_____

_____

_____

_____

Rainbow Flint Stone

Aids those who are feeling depressed or anxious. This beautiful stone will bring stability back into your life so you can enjoy the beauty your life has to offer. Because what you see is what you get! Choose this stone to get what you want. A super powerful healer!

Chakras: All

Fun Fact: Mined by the "Cool Guy" himself in Flint Ridge Ohio! The Native Americans used to make arrowheads from this flint. Often making more than they could carry back home; they would bury them until the next season. Upon their return they would dig them up. How did they remember where they had buried them? They planted a seedling tree on top of the location and knew how high the tree would grow making it easy to spot.

What insights, visions, words, understandings, perceptions, or awarenesses have I gained from my stone?

_____

_____

_____

_____

_____

_____

_____

_____

_____

_____

_____

_____

_____

_____

Rainforest Jasper

Hold this stone for flow, flow, flow. If you fight the flow, the flow will fight you. Step into the energy of flow and watch the magic happen. Share your magic with everyone you know. A truly purposeful stone!

Chakras: All

What insights, visions, words, understandings, perceptions, or awarenesses have I gained from my stone?

_____

_____

_____

_____

_____

_____

_____

_____

_____

_____

_____

_____

_____

_____

Red Butte Jasper

Gaze into this gorgeous stone. What do you see? Allow your eyes to soften for the messages this stone has to offer you. Metaphors are powerful messengers just like dreams. Allow this stone to help you remember and interpret your dreams too! Write your dreams down so you can revisit the messages for growth.

Chakras: heart, third eye, crown

What insights, visions, words, understandings, perceptions, or awarenesses have I gained from my stone?

_____

_____

_____

_____

_____

_____

_____

_____

_____

_____

_____

_____

_____

_____

Red Jasper

A powerful, grounding root chakra stone supporting your safety, security, family, money, home & job. These energies are so important and not to be overlooked. Paying attention is key. Good to keep with you all day.

Chakras: root, heart

What insights, visions, words, understandings, perceptions, or awarenesses have I gained from my stone?

_____

_____

_____

_____

_____

_____

_____

_____

_____

_____

_____

_____

_____

Red Moss Agate

A powerful stone for understanding opposites, such as people, or spectrums, such as politics, within your life. When it comes to discernment of polarization or opposition, mindfulness is key. A great earthy, grounding stone for proper decision-making and staying true to your beliefs.

Chakras: root, heart, throat

What insights, visions, words, understandings, perceptions, or awarenesses have I gained from my stone?

_____

_____

_____

_____

_____

_____

_____

_____

_____

_____

_____

_____

_____

_____

Red Ribbon Jasper

The ultimate grounding stone. When you feel all up in the air and are having trouble making decisions, use this stone. Hold tight, close your eyes and breathe deep. Let the right answer drop in directly from Spirit. It's really fun to practice this "answers from Spirit" whenever you can. As you get better and better, you know this stone is doing its job.

Chakras: root, third eye, crown

Fun Fact: This stone is mined in the upper peninsula of Michigan. The Cool Guy mines this one himself.

What insights, visions, words, understandings, perceptions, or awarenesses have I gained from my stone?

_____

_____

_____

_____

_____

_____

_____

_____

_____

_____

_____

_____

_____

_____

Red Tiger's Eye

The root chakra is red. Red is an abundant and powerful color. Let this stone help you in matters concerning home, family, safety, security, money and job. If you need help in any of these areas, hold this stone tight and ask for the help you need. Listen, see and feel what is transmitted to you through this stone and Spirit. The answers come quickly.

Chakras: root

What insights, visions, words, understandings, perceptions, or awarenesses have I gained from my stone?

_____

_____

_____

_____

_____

_____

_____

_____

_____

_____

_____

_____

_____

Red Zebra Lace Agate

A versatile stone which gives physical strength, stamina, compassion and understanding when needed throughout your day. Harmony and joy are also associated with this stone. Helps you see your gifts and use them in this world for good. A multifaceted stone!

Chakras: All

What insights, visions, words, understandings, perceptions, or awarenesses have I gained from my stone?

_____

_____

_____

_____

_____

_____

_____

_____

_____

_____

_____

_____

_____

_____

_____

Rhodochrosite

Such a sweet, sweet love stone. Use this stone in any relationship that needs a boost. Gift this stone to the person with whom you have a relationship with and/or put it close to you when in their presence. Remember not all relationships are romantic.

Chakras: root, heart

Shelly Norris

What insights, visions, words, understandings, perceptions, or awarenesses have I gained from my stone?

_____

_____

_____

_____

_____

_____

_____

_____

_____

_____

_____

_____

_____

_____

Rhodonite

A love stone! Aids in seeing the dark and light in your heart. Help to see the light that wins, and the dark can just be gone. A true challenge for many, but not with this stone!

Chakras: heart

What insights, visions, words, understandings, perceptions, or awarenesses have I gained from my stone?

_____

_____

_____

_____

_____

_____

_____

_____

_____

_____

_____

_____

_____

_____

Rose Quartz

Love amplified, clarified and magnified! Allow this stone to support you in opening your heart to all the people who drive you nuts. When you do this, watch their energy around you change as their hearts start to open up towards you. Remember: we all have a story that creates who we are today. Love heals all things.

Chakras: heart

What insights, visions, words, understandings, perceptions, or awarenesses have I gained from my stone?

_____

_____

_____

_____

_____

_____

_____

_____

_____

_____

_____

_____

_____

_____

Ruby in Zoisite

Sometimes love hides from us, but not with this stone! Ruby is the ultimate romantic love stone. The zoisite, which is green, allows your heart to open to romantic love - whether you're single or have been married for 30 years. A stone of passion in all areas of your life. Open up and say **YES** to love!

Chakras: heart

What insights, visions, words, understandings, perceptions, or awarenesses have I gained from my stone?

_____

_____

_____

_____

_____

_____

_____

_____

_____

_____

_____

_____

_____

_____

Rutilated Quartz

This stone is known as "On the wings of angels." Golden threads are plentiful as this stone connects us to our angels. Our angels are pure love and can only be just that. When you feel worried, anxious, fearful, or stressed let this stone summon your angels to help guide the way. Watch for their "signs" as they support you. You will feel their comfort quickly.

Chakras: root, heart, third eye, crown

What insights, visions, words, understandings, perceptions, or awarenesses have I gained from my stone?

_____

_____

_____

_____

_____

_____

_____

_____

_____

_____

_____

_____

_____

_____

Salmon Moonstone

Clarity! Do you ever feel called to the ocean when the moon is sparkling over the water? Or amongst the trees where the moon peeks through? Are you seeking guidance, answers, or the next right step? Let this stone remind you to go and find what you need within the comfort of Mother Nature. Clarity is a good feeling and important for our mental and emotional health.

Chakras: All

What insights, visions, words, understandings, perceptions, or awarenesses have I gained from my stone?

_____

_____

_____

_____

_____

_____

_____

_____

_____

_____

_____

_____

_____

_____

_____

Sardonyx

The stone of creativity in layers. As you step into creating the life you want, this stone reminds you to build it in layers. Or rather, put one foot in front of the other, take action and soon you'll be on your way! Hold this stone tight for the creative ideas that lead you in the direction of your heart. When you follow your heart, EVERYBODY wins.

Chakras: All

What insights, visions, words, understandings, perceptions, or awarenesses have I gained from my stone?

_____

_____

_____

_____

_____

_____

_____

_____

_____

_____

_____

_____

_____

_____

_____

_____

Shungite

An amazing healing stone for the physical body and mind. Wards off negative energy when used with positive intentions. An all-around powerful stone that comes in many shapes and sizes to suit your needs. Some of these stones are so small they'll fit in your water bottle and others are large enough to work in conjunction with your electronics.

Chakras: All

Fun Fact: Shungite has been used since the early 18th century for medicinal reasons; especially purified water. It has trace amounts of fullerenes which are antioxidants and the antibacterial properties have been confirmed by testing. It removes EMF's from your field caused by all things electronic. A group of scientists won a Nobel Prize for the discovery.

What insights, visions, words, understandings, perceptions, or awarenesses have I gained from my stone?

_____

_____

_____

_____

_____

_____

_____

_____

_____

_____

_____

_____

_____

_____

Smoky Quartz

For grounding and protection. A two for one! This gorgeous stone is meant to be near you, especially while at work or dealing with family triggers. It supports you when dealing with these matters, all the while helping you to not lose your mind. This can lead to potential destruction of relationships. So, keep a piece with you to save face and fall back in love or "like" with the people in your life. Remember baby steps: work miracles.

Chakras: root, throat, crown

What insights, visions, words, understandings, perceptions, or awarenesses have I gained from my stone?

_____

_____

_____

_____

_____

_____

_____

_____

_____

_____

_____

_____

_____

_____

Snakeskin Jasper

Feeling weighted down by others or life in general? This is a wonderful stone to help you release the things that don't serve you anymore so you can feel light again. Freedom can be achieved with this stone if you are ready. Are you ready? Let go of the heavy things and feel free.

Chakras: All

What insights, visions, words, understandings, perceptions, or awarenesses have I gained from my stone?

_____

_____

_____

_____

_____

_____

_____

_____

_____

_____

_____

_____

_____

_____

_____

Snowflake Obsidian

Grounding amplified when you most need it! Hold tight, close your eyes and just be in the moment. Feel yourself sink into the earth. Keeps away worry and depression.

Chakras: root, solar plexus, heart

What insights, visions, words, understandings, perceptions, or awarenesses have I gained from my stone?

_____

_____

_____

_____

_____

_____

_____

_____

_____

_____

_____

_____

_____

Sodalite

A stone of communication. Do you need help speaking your truth with kindness and grace? Do you get tongue-tied in front of certain people? Hold this stone to remind you of your power as well as your truth in all situations. Allow this stone to remove anger towards others as well, giving way to new forms of communication that serve your highest good and potential.

Chakras: root, throat

What insights, visions, words, understandings, perceptions, or awarenesses have I gained from my stone?

_____

_____

_____

_____

_____

_____

_____

_____

_____

_____

_____

_____

_____

_____

Speckled Epidote

Do you ever feel too airheaded or flighty like you're 'dropping things' or running into things and don't know why? Let this stone bring you back into your body so these feelings or actions go away. A great "bring you back into your body" stone when you hold tight and close your eyes and take some deep breaths and (of course) count to ten.

Chakras: root, crown

Fun Fact: This stone is mined by the Cool Guy himself!

What insights, visions, words, understandings, perceptions, or awarenesses have I gained from my stone?

_____

_____

_____

_____

_____

_____

_____

_____

_____

_____

_____

_____

_____

Spiderman Jasper

Use this stone to move forward by leaps and bounds. It will remind you of your talents and gifts given to you this lifetime. As you think of them you will smile, and your heart will open. This stone gently gives you the strength and courage to use your gifts for the highest good for yourself and others.

Chakras: root, solar plexus

What insights, visions, words, understandings, perceptions, or awarenesses have I gained from my stone?

_____

_____

_____

_____

_____

_____

_____

_____

_____

_____

_____

_____

_____

_____

Starburst Jasper

Encourages you to shine your light so bright that others can see their own light; therefore, helping them heal and live their best life. Aids you in being your magical self that the world recognizes and loves. A great healer's stone too.

Chakras: All

What insights, visions, words, understandings, perceptions, or awarenesses have I gained from my stone?

_____

_____

_____

_____

_____

_____

_____

_____

_____

_____

_____

_____

_____

_____

_____

Sunstone

Feeling down, alone, depressed sometimes? Allow this stone to brighten your day, not only by its beauty, but also its sparkly frequency. We all need some sparkle in our lives, especially when we feel icky. You can look at this stone from across the room or go over and pick it up for your sparkles. This will get you up and moving. Share it with others who need it too.

Chakras: root, solar plexus, heart, crown

What insights, visions, words, understandings, perceptions, or awarenesses have I gained from my stone?

_____

_____

_____

_____

_____

_____

_____

_____

_____

_____

_____

_____

_____

_____

_____

Tanzanite

A stone of royalty. Put your own invisible crown on and walk around like you own it! Stand tall and proud, feeling the vibration of the tanzanite in your own crown. A high frequency stone that supports you while you integrate its energy. Use it until you've mastered the feeling of royalty and then pass it on to another so they can benefit too.

Chakras: solar plexus, crown

Fun Fact: A stone from Africa and African royalty.

What insights, visions, words, understandings, perceptions, or awarenesses have I gained from my stone?

_____

_____

_____

_____

_____

_____

_____

_____

_____

_____

_____

_____

_____

_____

_____

Tiger Iron

A super-strong and powerful stone. Makes you feel "badass" about what you choose to do in your life. With this stone, bring in that feeling of "YES" I've got this! Protects from negative outside forces and cynics. Keep this energy close.

Chakras: root, sacral, solar plexus, heart

What insights, visions, words, understandings, perceptions or awareness's have I gained from my stone?

_____

_____

_____

_____

_____

_____

_____

_____

_____

_____

_____

_____

_____

_____

Topaz – Light Blue

A super-high frequency sweet stone. Let it help you take things to the next level with good intentions. Leave all unhelpfulness and ick behind with this stone. It gives you that feeling of "Love conquers all."

Chakras: solar plexus, heart, crown

What insights, visions, words, understandings, perceptions, or awarenesses have I gained from my stone?

_____

_____

_____

_____

_____

_____

_____

_____

_____

_____

_____

_____

_____

_____

Turritulla Agate

When you see signs of the ancient past, it is time to connect with your own past lives for massive healing. Seek a spiritual practitioner or a good book to help you through this process while holding this stone close.

Chakras: All

Fun Fact: This stone is mined by the Cool Guy himself! It is a conglomerate of fossil snail shells. From Wyoming and formed when the ocean covered this part of the world. Super cool!

What insights, visions, words, understandings, perceptions, or awarenesses have I gained from my stone?

_____

_____

_____

_____

_____

_____

_____

_____

_____

_____

_____

_____

_____

_____

_____

White Snakeskin Agate

How often do we all need to shed our old skin to reveal the new underneath? More often than we think, in order for massive forward movement! How brave are you to move as fast as the snake? Are you ready to shed your "skin" and move forward? This stone will support you now. Not only is it unique, like you, it knows how to assist in just this!

Chakras: All

What insights, visions, words, understandings, perceptions, or awarenesses have I gained from my stone?

_____

_____

_____

_____

_____

_____

_____

_____

_____

_____

_____

_____

_____

_____

Wonderstone

Aids in navigating life's ups and downs. Reminds you to keep putting one foot in front of the other for forward movement no matter how fast or slow. Encourages the energy of "You've got this!" Also, a great stone for bringing more miracles, blessings and abundance into your life by simply asking the Universe. Ask for what you want not what you don't want. Keep close when needed.

Chakras: All

Fun Fact: This stone is mined by the Cool Guy himself!

What insights, visions, words, understandings, perceptions, or awarenesses have I gained from my stone?

_____

_____

_____

_____

_____

_____

_____

_____

_____

_____

_____

_____

_____

_____

_____

Yellow Jasper

The "Do Something" stone. Stimulates your solar plexus chakra, increasing your intuition, while supporting you in taking action to move your life in the direction you desire. Keep this stone close when your motivation starts to dwindle, and you need a kick in the pants to remember why you do what you do. You get one life in this body, make it your best by taking action and doing something!

Chakras: All, especially solar plexus

What insights, visions, words, understandings, perceptions, or awarenesses have I gained from my stone?

_____

_____

_____

_____

_____

_____

_____

_____

_____

_____

_____

_____

_____

_____

_____

Zebra Jasper

A brilliant balancing stone for those who feel "being" can be too much. Allows you to see the softer side of life more often and to let go and relax. So proclaim your release and kick your feet up more often!

Chakras: root, third eye, crown

What insights, visions, words, understandings, perceptions, or awarenesses have I gained from my stone?

_____

_____

_____

_____

_____

_____

_____

_____

_____

_____

_____

_____

_____

_____

_____

Zebra Quartz

When you feel off balance and your world is spinning off its axis, grab this high frequency stone to stabilize your mind and heart. Allow your mind and heart to sync up in a balanced way for you to put your best foot forward. Start skipping or 'dance it out' right back into balance.

Chakras: root, heart, crown

What insights, visions, words, understandings, perceptions, or awarenesses have I gained from my stone?

_____

_____

_____

_____

_____

_____

_____

_____

_____

_____

_____

_____

_____

_____

The stones used to write this book came from Shelly's Rock Shop, LLC.

Find me on Facebook at
https://www.facebook.com/shellysrockshop/

Find me on Instagram at
https://www.instagram.com/shellynorris15/

Email me at shellyrocks888@gmail.com

Disclaimer: It is important that I say this - under no circumstances do I claim that these stones alone can heal you, fix you or guide you without taking your own action steps. The energy or frequency of these stones simply serve as a nudging reminder to use your own intuition and do what is best for you.

Shelly Norris

Shelly Norris

Made in the USA
San Bernardino, CA
26 December 2019

62344297R00146